How to Draw
Amazing
Birds

from Songbirds to Birds of Prey

BARRON'S

Created and produced by Green Android Ltd

Illustrated by Fiona Gowen

First edition for The United States and Canada
published in 2017 by
Barron's Educational Series, Inc.

Copyright © Green Android Ltd 2017

Green Android Ltd
49 Beaumont Court
Upper Clapton Road
London, E5 8BG
www.greenandroid.co.uk

All inquiries should be addressed to:
Barron's Educational Series, Inc.
250 Wireless Boulevard
Hauppauge, NY 11788
www.barronseduc.com

ISBN: 978-1-4380-1053-3
Library of Congress Control No: 2017932828

Date of Manufacture:
April 2017
Manufactured by:
Toppan Leefung Printing Co., Ltd.
Shenzhen, China

Printed in China
9 8 7 6 5 4 3 2 1

Contents

Page 32 has an index of everything to draw in this book.

Perching Songbirds

There are about 4,000 species of songbirds. Each one has a vocal organ that produces elaborate song to signal territory, identity, or courtship.

1 Draw the head and the beak. Then, draw the throat and the breast.

2 Pencil in a large eye, the back, and the wings.

3 Draw the tail and the ruffled thighs.

4 Draw the legs, toes, claws, and top of the branch.

More to Draw

Songbirds are found in open grasslands and forests.
The best songsters are nightingales, larks, and thrushes.

5 Add texture to the throat, breast, and wing. Draw the ear covert—the feather that covers the ear (left of eye).

Song Thrush

6 Finish by adding shading to the body and wing, and then strengthen the outlines.

Nightingale

Blue Jay

Swallow

American Tree Sparrow

Japanese White-eye

Blue Mockingbird

Crested Lark

Cedar Waxwing

Desert Cardinal

European Robin

This well-known bird is famed for its red face and breast. When cold, it puffs out its feathers for added warmth. During its short, fast flights, its wings beat rapidly.

1 Draw the head, nape, and pointed beak. Then, draw the throat and the breast.

2 Pencil a circle for an eye and fill it in. Add detail to the beak, and draw the back, the wing, and the belly.

3 Draw the legs, each ending with three forward-pointing clawed toes and one rear-pointing clawed toe. Draw the ground.

6

European Robin

4 Draw the upward-pointing tail.

5 Sketch light, broken lines to define the red breast, and add texture to the wings.

6 Finish by adding shading. Then, strengthen the main outlines.

How to Draw
Precious Penguins

These flightless birds, found in the Southern Hemisphere, spend 75 percent of their time hunting in the water. Their time on land is spent breeding, caring for young, and moulting.

1 Draw the head, bill, and eye. Then, draw the neck and the belly.

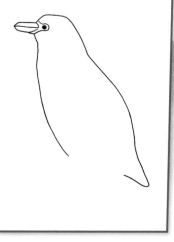

2 Pencil the penguin's back and wedge-shaped tail.

3 Pencil in both flippers. Note that they are halfway down the body.

4 Draw the legs and the webbed feet. Each foot has three forward-pointing claws.

More to Draw

There are 17 species of penguins. The largest is the emperor penguin; the smallest is the little blue penguin.

5 Add light lines and dots to define the penguin's markings.

Adélie Penguin

Macaroni Penguin

Chinstrap Penguin

Emperor Penguin

Humboldt Penguin

Rockhopper Penguin

6 Finish by adding shading to the neck and the chest. Strengthen the outlines.

King Penguin

Little Blue Penguin

Gentoo Penguin

African Penguin

9

How to Draw
Pointy Pelican

This giant waterbird has a long, pointed bill and a large throat pouch that scoops up water and prey, like fish, frogs, turtles, and prawns. The water is drained before the prey are swallowed.

1 Draw the head and its fluffy crest. Then, draw the neck, long bill, throat, and chest.

2 Pencil in the eye and circle it. Add detail to the bill. Draw the back, tail, and thigh.

3 Draw the wings and complete the tail.

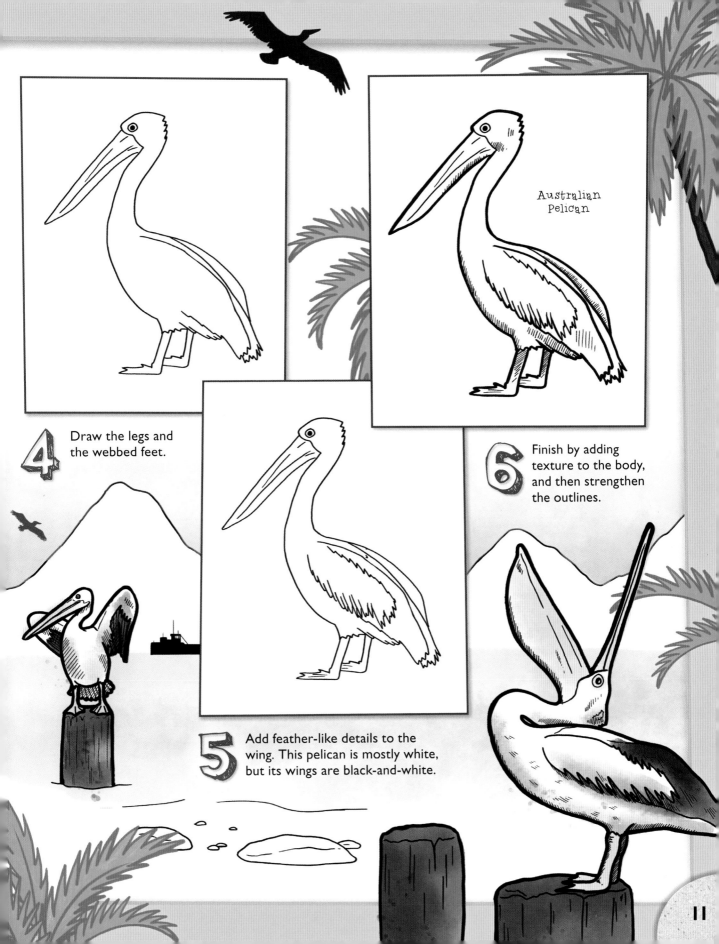

Australian Pelican

4 Draw the legs and the webbed feet.

5 Add feather-like details to the wing. This pelican is mostly white, but its wings are black-and-white.

6 Finish by adding texture to the body, and then strengthen the outlines.

How to Draw

Birds of Prey

Also known as raptors, which means "to seize," these birds have amazing vision even at high speeds. They also have powerful talons and hooked beaks. Their broad wings allow them to soar.

1 Draw the leading edge of the wings and the head, beak, neck, and chest.

2 Pencil in an eye. Then, draw a wiggly line for the tail feathers.

3 Add the finger-like primary and secondary feathers to the trailing edges of both wings.

4 Draw the feathered legs, which each have three front toes with talons. Draw a rear-facing toe and a talon on each foot.

The smallest raptor measures just 6 inches (15 cm), while the bald eagle can have up to a 7.5 foot (2.5 m) wingspan.

5 Add detail to the wings and legs, and draw zigzag lines on the neck and the chest.

Golden Eagle

6 Finish by shading the wings, body, and legs. Then, strengthen the outline of this powerful bird.

Osprey

Australian Hobby

Merlin

Sparrowhawk

Bald Eagle

Crested Caracara

Peregrine Falcon

Steller's Sea Eagle

Secretary Bird

How to Draw

Zebra Finch

The zebra finch is the most common finch in Australia. It has a red, cone-shaped beak and distinctive zebra-like markings. The male has chestnut-colored cheeks.

1 Draw the head, beak, throat, and breast.

2 Add the back, tail, and belly. Pencil in the eye, and circle it. Then, add the nostril, neck and beak detail.

3 Draw a "V" shape on the cheek for the male's marking. Draw the wings.

14

4 Pencil in the feathered thighs and legs. Draw its clawed toes wrapped around a branch.

5 Draw feathers on the wings and zebra-like stripes on the tail. Pencil face markings and dots on the chest.

Zebra Finch

6 Add shading to the body and legs and fill in alternate stripes on the tail. Finish by strengthening the outlines.

How to Draw
Stealthy Owls

Most owls hunt under the cover of darkness. Their dull coloration and almost silent flight allows them to surprise their prey of small mammals, insects, fish, and other birds.

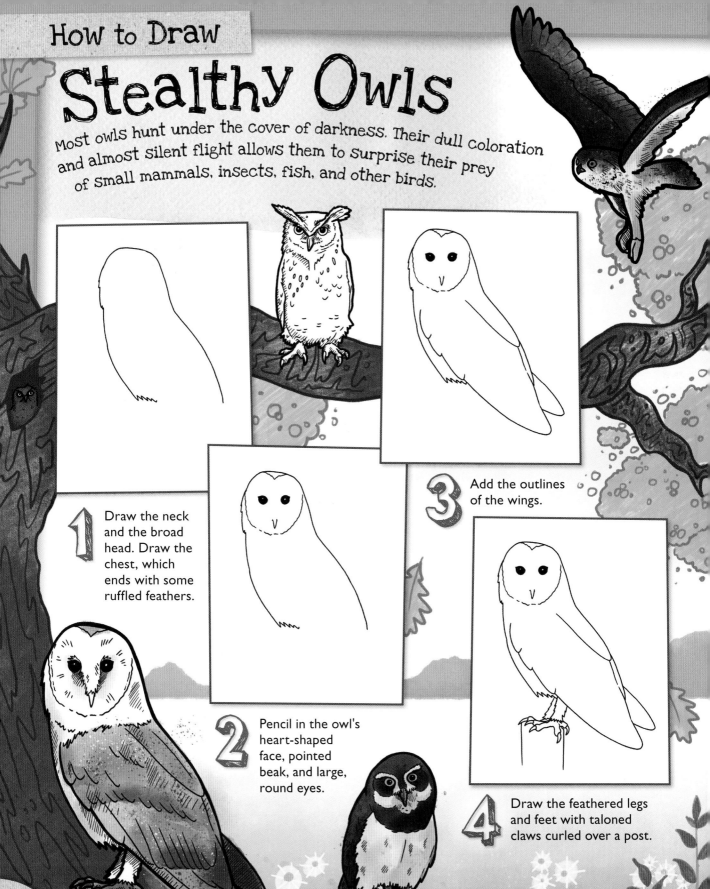

1 Draw the neck and the broad head. Draw the chest, which ends with some ruffled feathers.

2 Pencil in the owl's heart-shaped face, pointed beak, and large, round eyes.

3 Add the outlines of the wings.

4 Draw the feathered legs and feet with taloned claws curled over a post.

More to Draw

There are 200 species of owls. All have a broad head, upright stance, and excellent sight and hearing.

Cape Eagle-owl

Oriental Bay Owl

Snowy Owl

Long-eared Owl

Great Horned Owl

Tawny Owl

Spectacled Owl

Burrowing Owl

Northern Pygmy Owl

5 Pencil detail on the face, neck, and post. Add feathering to the wings.

Barn Owl

6 Finish by lightly shading the owl's body and legs, and then strengthen the outlines.

Shy Kingfisher

Although the colorful kingfisher avoids humans, it is regarded as an omen of good luck. The dagger-like beak is designed to aid those species that hunt fish.

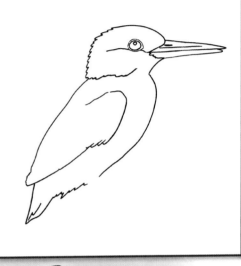

1 Sketch the neck, head, pointed beak, throat, and chest.

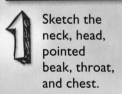

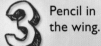

2 Draw the eye and add detail to the head and the beak. Then, draw the back and the tail.

3 Pencil in the wing.

4 Draw the legs with the claws gripping a rock.

Common Kingfisher

5 Sketch in the distinctive plumage and markings on the head and wing. Add texture to the chest, and fill in the eye.

6 Finish by shading the head, body, and rock. Strengthen the outlines.

How to Draw
Birds from Sea to Shore

The mute swan is a waterfowl and it is the largest of the swans. It is recognized by its all-white feathers and black-edged bill, which is crowned with a large bulge.

1 Draw the head and the pronounced bulge. Then, draw the bill, throat, and long neck.

2 Draw the swan's body sitting on the rippling water. Draw an eye, and add detail to the bill.

3 Draw the large wings with their feathered trailing edges. Draw the thigh.

More to Draw

All these birds live in freshwater or saltwater habitats.
Some have webbed feet, others have clawed toes.

Greylag Goose

Canada Goose

4 Draw the primary feathers and the tail.

Common Loon

5 Add detail to the wings and to the primary feathers.

Mute Swan

African Darter

Mandarin Duck

Grey Heron

Atlantic Puffin

6 Finish by adding shading. Strengthen the outlines.

Shoebill Stork

Common Moorhen

Greater Flamingo

Although the flamingo is best known for its coloring, long neck, and spindly legs, it is also an excellent swimmer. The flamingo is pink because its diet consists mainly of small shrimp.

1 Draw the head and the large, bent beak. Then, draw the throat, long neck, and chest.

2 Draw the remainder of the neck, and then draw the back and tail. Draw an eye.

3 Sketch in a wing, and complete the tail.

4 Draw the standing leg, starting at the thigh, with a knee and a webbed foot. Draw the raised leg.

5 Sketch in the feathers on the wing. Fill the beak tip with black.

Greater Flamingo

6 To finish, strengthen the outlines, and add shading to the body and legs.

How to Draw
Playful Parrots

There are over 390 species of parrots, and many are kept as lively and intelligent pets. The African grey parrot is known as the "Einstein" parrot because of its talking ability.

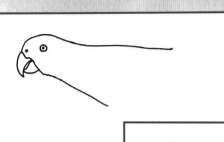

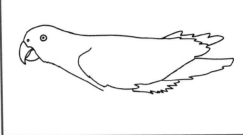

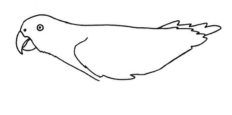

1 Draw the head and back. Then, draw the beak, throat, and chest. Draw a nostril and an eye.

2 Pencil in the parrot's wings.

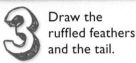

3 Draw the ruffled feathers and the tail.

4 Draw the thighs and the legs. Draw the feet, each with two forward-facing toes and two rear-facing toes.

More to Draw

Parrots live in tropical regions and most are colorful.
They range in size from 3–40 inches (8–100 cm)!

5 Add detail to the wings, tail, and thighs, and pencil markings to the head, face, neck, throat, and chest.

6 Finish by shading the lower body, thighs, legs, wings, and tail. Strengthen the outlines.

Swift
Parrot

Palm
Cockatoo

Black-headed
Parrot

Red-crowned
Amazon

Hyacinth
Macaw

African
Grey Parrot

Parakeet

Kea

Galah

Rainbow
Lorikeet

How to Draw

Birds on Parade

Almost every bird performs some sort of display, mostly during courtship—when trying to find a mate. A display can include postures, elaborate fanning or plumping of feathers, and sounds.

1 Draw the head, face, beak, and neck. Sketch in the crest on the top of the head.

2 Pencil the chest and the body.

3 Draw thighs and legs. Draw the feet, which have three forward-facing toes and one rear-facing toe.

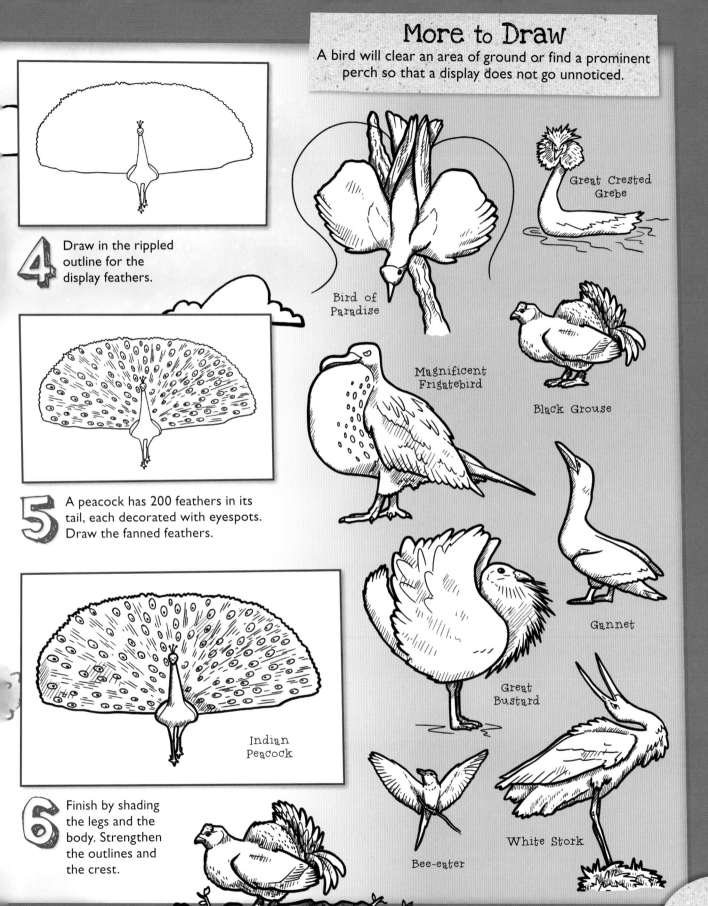

More to Draw

A bird will clear an area of ground or find a prominent perch so that a display does not go unnoticed.

4 Draw in the rippled outline for the display feathers.

5 A peacock has 200 feathers in its tail, each decorated with eyespots. Draw the fanned feathers.

6 Finish by shading the legs and the body. Strengthen the outlines and the crest.

Indian Peacock

Bird of Paradise

Great Crested Grebe

Magnificent Frigatebird

Black Grouse

Gannet

Great Bustard

Bee-eater

White Stork

How to Draw
Keel-billed Toucan

This fruit-eating bird of Southern Mexico and northern South America has a large—about one-third the length of its body—and colorful bill. Its tongue measures 6 inches (15 cm)!

1 Draw the head, neck, and bill. Draw an eye.

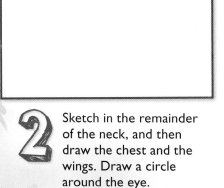

2 Sketch in the remainder of the neck, and then draw the chest and the wings. Draw a circle around the eye.

3 Draw claws—two forward-facing ones on each foot—gripping the branch. Add the ruffled feathers under the beak.

5 Add detail to the bill, and outline the marking on its face and throat.

4 Draw the toucan's tail. Other than its colorful bill and face, this bird is glossy black.

Keel-billed
Toucan

6 Finish by shading the chin, chest, wings, and tail. Strengthen the outlines.

How to Draw

Record-breaking Birds

The ostrich is the largest bird, but it also lays the largest eggs. Although the ostrich has wings, they are too weak to support flight. This bird is built for sprinting.

1 Draw the head, beak, and eye. Then, draw the throat and the long neck.

2 Sketch in the body using a wriggly line to represent its feathers.

3 Pencil in a wing, and roughly sketch the tail.

4 Draw the left thigh and leg with its two-toed foot, and then draw the right leg.

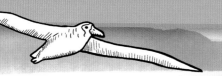

The seven birds featured below are exceptional for their body or beak size or their weight or wingspan.

5 Add detail to the legs and the neck. Sketch feathers on the body, wings, and tail.

6 Add shading, especially to the lower body, and then strengthen the outlines.

Southern Cassowary

Emu

Wandering Albatross

Greater Rhea

Common ostrich

Kori Bustard

Andean Condor

Dalmatian Pelican

Index

This index is in alphabetical order, and it lists all the birds that are featured in this book so that you can easily find your favorites.

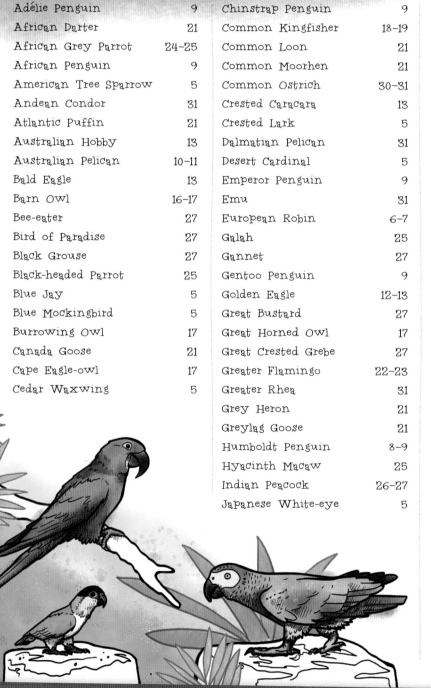